The Prestige S

Midland Rea

John Banks
Photography by G H F Atkins

© 2003 J M Banks

ISBN 1 898432 88 0

Cover: Three generations of Midland Red double-deckers: a D7, a D9 and a Daimler Fleetline,
photographed at Leicester in August 1970, 18 or so months into NBC ownership.

Rear cover: A good selection of Midland Red vehicles in artist's impressions on the cover of a 1941
timetable. *(Courtesy John Senior)*

Title page: The enthusiast living outside Midland Red's operating area was not spared the
"strangeness" of the fleet, for its vehicles were encountered on long distance express services,
particularly in London, and on tours, excursions and private hire assignments throughout the
country. Midland Red coaches of the early postwar period were handsome, dignified machines,
well ahead of their time in appearance and technical specification. Number **3323** (**KHA 323**) was
one of a batch of 45 BMMO C1s with centre-entrance 30-seat coachwork by Duple. It is seen at
Victoria coach station in August 1950. It had entered service the previous year and was withdrawn
in 1964, serving thence as a driver-trainer until sold for scrap in April 1975.

Opposite page: The C1's contemporary as a stage-carriage service bus was the BMMO S9, of
which there was a batch of 100 built in 1949/50 with 40-seat front-entrance bodywork by Brush.
This May 1949 view inside Brush's Loughborough factory shows a line of new S9s headed by No.
3416 (**LHA 416**) almost ready for despatch to Midland Red. All 100 of this batch of S9s were
lengthened and reseated to 44 by Charles H Roe, of Crossgates, Leeds, in 1952.

Below: Midland Red's was a homogeneous fleet; there was nonetheless much variety, as in this trio
photographed at rest at Birmingham Digbeth in August 1959. On the left is No. **4006** (**SHA 406**),
a 1953 Leyland PD2/20 Titan with Leyland 56-seat highbridge rear-entrance bodywork; in the
centre is No. **2353** (**FHA 857**), which dated from 1939 and was an SOS FEDD. Also a 56-seater,
but with Brush bodywork and to forward-entrance specification, 2353 lasted until 1960 after a
rebuild by Hooton in 1951. Alongside it is a Metro-Cammell-bodied 63-seat rear-entrance BMMO
D7, No. **4524** (**XHA 524**). This one was withdrawn in 1970 and scrapped the following year.

INTRODUCTION

One summer evening in the early 1970s, a party from a Midland Red garage came to a social event at the headquarters of Northampton Corporation Transport. Onto the forecourt of a depot containing nothing but Roe-bodied Daimler CVG6 double-deckers with half-cabs and open rear platforms, drew a Midland Red D9. During the course of the visit a constant stream of Northampton platform staff - and these were busmen by profession, not necessarily enthusiasts - wandered over to the D9 to spend time inspecting it.

That perhaps sums up what it was about the Birmingham & Midland Motor Omnibus Company's fleet: even hard-bitten drivers and conductors at the end, or in the middle, of a shift were drawn by the character and quality of the visiting vehicle. The writer recalls that many of the comments passed were on the lines of "wish we had some of these..."

It was, and is, extraordinarily difficult to explain that character and quality. Midland Red vehicles down the decades were always highly individual and some of the earlier types often had an archaic appearance that belied their technical excellence and sophistication of construction: a trait shared - in perhaps the closest comparison of which one can think - by much of the contemporary Paris fleet. On the other hand, there were also vehicles that were in advance of their time in styling and appearance.

Much of the reason for this stems from the majority of Midland Red vehicles having been home made, though that homely expression scarcely does justice to the major engineering operation that the Company built up to provide itself with both chassis and bodies.

The Company's start in 1904, when the Birmingham Motor Express Co Ltd registered the Birmingham and Midland Motor Omnibus Company Ltd as a separate venture, was not immediately followed by in-house vehicle building and the BMMO had been in existence as a provider of passenger transport services for around two decades before it turned to manufacturing its own vehicles. By the early 1920s the fleet was based upon petrol-electric chassis of Tilling-Stevens manufacture. The petrol-electric system, wherein a petrol engine drove an electric motor that supplied power to the transmission, is said to have been chosen because horse-bus drivers would adapt more easily to such a "gearless" system - shades of fully automatic Routemasters a generation later for London trolleybus drivers.

In a souvenir brochure put out by the Company in 1964, it was suggested that it had decided around 1923 to build its own chassis because it could find no proprietary British vehicle with which to combat competition from small operators using nimble, lightweight

Above: Photographed as late as September 1988, the "Midland" device above the portal of Southgate Street garage, Leicester, was typical of many such proud examples of company identity that had survived the decades.

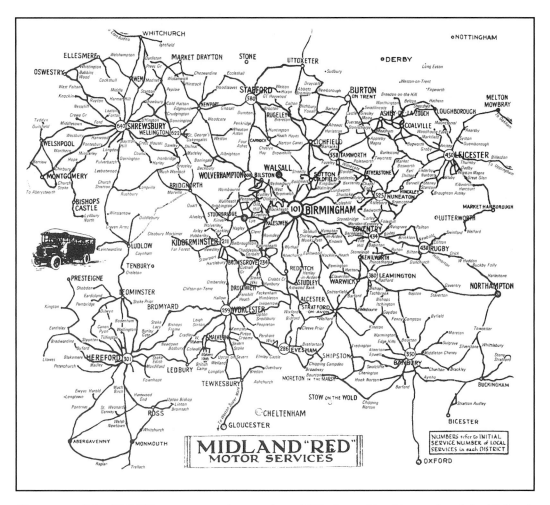

The extent of the BMMO's route network as early as 1925. A considerable swathe of the Midlands was shown on the map as being available to passengers using the Company's services: diagonally from Bicester to Oswestry or Melton Mowbray to Abergavenny, or north to south from Uttoxeter to Gloucester - "where there are no through buses, convenient connections are arranged" claimed Company publicity. (Courtesy John Senior)

vehicles, often of American manufacture, running on pneumatic tyres. The Midland Red workshops, consequent upon that decision, built a prototype, known as "SOS". Nobody knows for what the letters SOS stood. The most likely meaning seems to be "Superior Omnibus Specification". Whatever it meant, SOS was the name given to BMMO-built chassis before the war; afterwards they were known simply as "BMMO".

The SOS designation, born as a lightweight, pneumatic-tyred single-decker, came in the prewar period to embrace most types of passenger carrying vehicle: *chars-à-bancs*,

coaches, larger single-deckers and double-deckers and even a rear-engined prototype. From those small beginnings, by the outbreak of the second world war, the Edgbaston and Bearwood workshops would turn out, in some 30 different types and sub-types, nearly 3,000 chassis, of which approximately a third were supplied to other operators.

And they were needed: already by 1924 Midland Red vehicles were carrying 34 million passengers annually and running more than ten million miles to do so; expansion in the latter half of the twenties and into the next decade was rapid, however, as it was in the same

5

period for many another established operator, and by 1934 the fleet of just over 300 vehicles had increased to over a thousand.

That threefold increase in a decade had been fuelled by such advances as taking over the city services in Worcester and many others between centres of population, all of which resulted in Midland Red's territory stretching from Shrewsbury in the west to Leicester in the east, and from Stafford and Burton-on-Trent down to Hereford and Banbury.

During this same decade the BMMO came under the influence of the Great Western and London, Midland & Scottish railway companies. Long distance work was not new at that time - 1930 - but Midland Red's involvement took a major step forward when Black & White Motorways, of Cheltenham, was purchased. Control of the new acquisition was shared with two other operators and in 1934 the BMMO was prominent in plans to create the Associated Motorways coordination scheme (see Prestige Series No. 18 *"Associated Motorways"*).

Before the provisions of the Road Traffic Act, 1930 began to be felt, Midland Red simply ran services in competition with established operators and hoped to come off best. After the

Act, however, and in the face of the powers wielded by the newly created Traffic Commissioners, it was necessary to buy out competing operators, whose businesses, by virtue of the licences now held for their services, had assumed a value; as a consequence some 150 businesses were bought adding many new services to Midland Red's own network; all this expansion meant that additional garage and administrative premises were concomitantly added to the Company's empire. Seldom were acquired businesses' vehicles taken into the BMMO operational fleet, though this was not unknown.

The outbreak of war brought an end to production of SOS chassis and the Chief Engineer, L G Wyndham Shire, who had been largely responsible for the long series of SOS types, retired in 1940. Most of the vehicles added to the fleet in the war years were of necessity of types quite alien to Midland Red. The Ministry of Supply laid down a somewhat austere specification to which chassis and bodywork manufacturers had to adhere, and such vehicles - known widely as "austerities" or "utilities" - were all that were available to operators until better times came as the austerity years that succeeded the hostilities

Above: It was common for companies to show their pride in their operation by producing letter-headed notepaper that was a work of art in itself. Bus operators often included a drawing of one of their latest vehicles, and for that reason the design had to be regularly updated. This early thirties BMMO example makes much of the recent involvement of the railway companies - their erstwhile competitors. (Courtesy John Senior)

gave way to a period of postwar optimism. For a short time at the beginning of the war there was a type of chassis known as "unfrozen", where vehicles were produced from stocks of parts already in existence from the prewar period - sometimes, indeed, such vehicles had been already partly constructed when construction of buses had been halted as an emergency measure on war's outbreak.

Wartime vehicles thus acquired were on Leyland Titan, AEC Regent II, Guy Arab and Daimler CWA6 chassis, carrying a variety of bodywork - none of them bore much resemblance to Midland Red SOS products.

After the war was over the Company began to manufacture its own vehicles again at its Carlyle Road premises although, as we have mentioned, they were henceforth known as BMMO rather than as SOS. The legendary "D" and "S" series for double- and single-deckers came first, soon followed by the "C" series used for coaches. By the time BMMO's own production ceased, these series had reached D10, S23 and C6 respectively.

From time to time the Company found that it could not build enough vehicles for its needs and proprietary makes were bought, mainly from Leyland Motors Ltd, though Guy and AEC were also favoured and latterly the Daimler Fleetline was purchased in some numbers. In some cases its own chassis were found in need of rebodying and outside coachbuilders were again employed.

Much of Midland Red's story in the 1950s and 1960s reflects that of other large operators: falling traffic caused by the growth of private motoring; the popularity of television removing much of the evening cinema patronage; the consequent need to increase fares and thus drive away even more passengers; and the difficulties of introducing one-man operation as it was then known.

One event, though, that brought the Company into renewed prominence came in 1959 when the M1 motorway between Birmingham and London was opened and Midland Red provided an express service using the new road between the two cities. By then the C series for coaches had reached C5, a design that was modified for high-speed running with a turbocharged engine and a new gearbox. The resulting vehicles, known as the CM5T type, were capable of 85mph and with them it was possible to provide an end-to-end service of 2 hours 55 minutes, not much more than half of the pre-motorway time of 5 hours 20 minutes. It is not often that the word "sensation" can justifiably be used of public road transport, but the BMMO caused one with the introduction of the CM5Ts.

In the meantime the Company's more mundane service buses were achieving an advanced technical specification. The D9 double-decker appeared in 1958 and some of the reasons for the interest in it displayed by the professional busmen described at the start of this introduction centred round its variable-rate rubber suspension (already in use on BMMO single-deckers and coaches), independent front suspension, 10.5-litre engine, semi-automatic transmission with fingertip gear selection and two-pedal control. The design incorporated much use of fibreglass panels and as a 72-seater it was welcomed by traffic management. Several hundred D9s were built and it was Midland Red's swan-song so far as double-deckers were concerned, for the even more sophisticated chassisless, underfloor-engined, 78-seat D10 of 1961 was stillborn.

The British Electric Traction Co Ltd had not taken to kindly to the idea of becoming part of a nationalised bus operating concern and had made its stance well known. It came as something of a surprise, therefore, when in 1967 BET's shareholdings were acquired by the state-owned Transport Holding Company, an event that paved the way for Midland Red to become a THC company and, not long afterwards, part of the National Bus Company, which came into being on 1st January 1969.

The latter event, which was to bring new liveries, logos and vehicle policies, seemed a natural point at which to terminate coverage of the fleet in this book.

Acknowledgements

The writer would find it difficult to overestimate the contribution to his writings on the British bus scene made by his friend of many years, Ron Maybray, whose extensive written records have provided data not easily obtainable elsewhere. This and many others of the books in the *Prestige* and *Super Prestige* series have benefited from Ron's meticulous and ungrudgingly given assistance: a debt that is gratefully acknowledged; as indeed is that to The PSV Circle and The Omnibus Society, whose excellent publications aimed at the enthusiast are indispensable.

To John Senior thanks for allowing use of the map, the letter-heading, the timetable cover and the inside front cover pictures, the latter from the brush of G S Cooper, all of which first appeared in *Midland Red Volume 1*, published a quarter of a century ago by the Transport Publishing Company.

Paul Gray has cast an expert eye over the text and made numerous welcome suggestions for its improvement; David and Mary Shaw have as always looked after the proof-reading.

All the pictures in this book and that on the front cover were taken by the Nottingham-based transport photographer, Geoffrey Atkins, whose work will be well known to readers of earlier volumes in this series. Geoffrey has a particular love of the Midland Red fleet, and has taken more pictures of it than of any other. Although now, in his 92nd year, no longer active behind the camera or in the dark room, and having now passed much of his material into the care of the writer, for three quarters of a century, from 1927 to 2002, Geoffrey was an avid recorder of the public transport scene, particularly in and around his Nottingham base.

A large proportion of the Atkins Midland Red views were taken in Leicester, easily visited from the photographer's home, in pursuance of Geoffrey's desire to record the art of the coachbuilder. Ever fascinated by the latter, he had as a young man wished to enter the coachbuilding industry himself. Denied the opportunity, he nonetheless set about creating a unique visual record of bus and coach bodywork from all the major and many of the minor coachbuilders. Thus, to some extent, the identity of a vehicle, its location and the route on which it was running were secondary considerations in his photographs.

As so often with these volumes, no claim is made that either a definitive history or a fleet list is being offered: rather is the book the frame for another fine selection of pictures from the cameras of Geoffrey Atkins.

John Banks
Romiley, Cheshire
February 2003

The BMMO standards - the 36ft-long service bus, in this case an S22, and a D9 72-seat double-decker - as the Company approached being swallowed up by the National Bus Company - are seen side by side in an October 1968 picture at Digbeth.

Above: One of the earliest Atkins Midland Red pictures, taken with a Kodak Vest Pocket camera using Kodak "non-curling" film, dates from July 1928 at Weston Super Mare. The rather stately Carlyle (BMMO)-bodied 30-seater is an SOS QC type, No. **721 (HA 3671)**, a 1927 machine that was withdrawn in 1935.

Below: At the Queens Road terminus in Nottingham, near the Great Central Railway bridge, **972 (HA 4909)** was photographed in September 1930. This was a 1929 Brush-bodied 34-seat SOS M type, which lasted in service until 1947. This was the only one of the 49 M types in the Midland Red fleet to have a Brush body, rather than either BMMO or Ransomes.

Page 10: Built in 1927, with a Carlyle 37-seat body, **674 (HA 3600)**, an SOS Q type, did not have front-wheel brakes when new. By the time of this August 1933 view at Grantham it had been so fitted. The vehicle was withdrawn in 1936.

Page 11: **734 (HA 3675)**, a Carlyle-bodied 30-seat SOS QC type, was on the Birmingham to Nottingham service when spotted at Huntingdon Street bus station, Nottingham, in March 1934. Then six years old, it was withdrawn the following year and sold to Northern General.

<< *Opposite page:* The "Midland Red Motor Services" lettering boldly cast into the top and bottom of the radiator made up for the lack of the "Midland" fleetname transfer on the Q-type coaches; a crest being favoured instead. **789** (**HA 4822**), a Short Bros-bodied 29-seat QLC type, was at Prince George Street, Skegness, in July 1929. HA 4822 was sold to Northern General in 1935.

Above: Fitted with Ransomes 37-seat bodywork, **900** (**HA 4840**), an SOS QL type, was at Skegness in July 1930. In 1935 this vehicle was reseated to 35, was impressed by the War Department in 1940, returned to Midland Red in 1942 and was then scrapped.

Below: **1065** (**HA 4972**), an SOS XL type with Brush coachwork, was photographed *en route* for Bournemouth in 192930. It was one of a batch, 1045-87, whose lightweight SOS chassis were inadequate for such heavy, luxuriously appointed long-distance coachwork. All were converted to six-cylinder MM types and fitted with bodies from or intended for other chassis and received revised registration numbers in the HA 5xxx series, this one becoming HA 5015.

Above: The IM and IM4 types of SOS constructed between 1930 and 1934 were good performers, despite being fitted with four-cylinder petrol engines of no more than 4.3 litres. The type in original condition is exemplified by **1263** (**HA 6192**), seen at Huntingdon Street, Nottingham, in August 1933 whilst working the X99 express service to Birmingham. Some of these vehicles were adaptations of earlier chassis, but HA 6192 was one of the first production batch, which in 1931 introduced a revised outline of radiator with a flat top. The 34-seat body was by Short Bros and the vehicle was commandeered by the War Department in 1940 and did not return to Midland Red.

>> *Opposite page upper:* This picture, another service X99 view taken at Huntingdon Street bus station in Nottingham, this time in August 1934, tells the other side of the story outlined on page 13 in connection with the batch 1045-87, and shows an MM (6 cylinder) type, **1057** (**HA 5130**), after the rebodying (by Ransomes) and reregistration. As an XL type, it had been registered HA 4967. In this form the vehicle lasted until 1950.

>> *Opposite page lower:* By 1931 the Midland Red fleet had become entirely single-deck but in that year, to answer a need for larger-capacity vehicles on busy services in the industrial Black Country, a prototype SOS DD model rear-entrance double-decker was built, to be followed by fifty production versions. When forward-entrance double-deckers followed in 1934, the model designation of the earlier buses was changed to DD (RE), soon universally known as the REDD. Ten of the production DDs had metal-framed 52-seat bodywork by the Metropolitan-Cammell Carriage & Wagon Company, epitomised by brand new **1391** (**HA 8048**) seen in Leicester in August 1933. The production batch of 50 was 1370-419, bodied by four different coachbuilders: Short Bros, Eastern Counties, Brush and MCCW. This picture provides an example of Midland Red's dual numbering system in that period. All "fleet" numbers quoted in this book are in fact from BMMO's chronologically sequential "Private Identification Numbers" (PINs, well in advance of widespread use of such things!); however, most vehicles up to the year 1944 also had "bonnet" numbers. The latter coincided with the registration numbers but when three-letter registrations came in the system could not but throw up bonnet number duplication. There was in any case a reluctance to allocate four-digit bonnet numbers, although these double-deckers had them, and HA 8048, in addition to its private identification number 1391, carried the bonnet number **1048** until 1944.

15

The 1933 prototype SOS LRR, 1499 (HA 9051), had a BMMO 6.373-litre petrol engine and five-speed gearbox and was a very sprightly performer. The Short Bros body had 30 coach seats, later converted as a 34-seat bus. It was at Victoria coach station in September 1934.

HA 9051 *(see p. 16)* was the prototype for a 1934/5 batch of 30 LRR coaches, but differed in many respects from them and was never, as a coach, updated, always retaining its experimental status. **1651 (AHA 596)** represents the production batch, which were also Short Bros 30-seat coaches, similarly converted as 34-seat service buses in 1940/1, at which time the prototype was modified to to match the production vehicles. In this August 1940 picture at Union Road, Nottingham, wartime livery modifications and masked headlamps are evident.

<< *Opposite page:* Midland Red introduced its ON chassis in 1934 to take advantage of the then permitted maximum length of 27ft 6ins for two-axle single-deckers. The compact SOS 5.986-litre RR2SB petrol engine allowed a seating capacity of no fewer than 38. Three of the buses (the first series was HA 9451-86) were built with the AEC 7.7-litre diesel engine, which - because of its greater length - resulted in a lower seating capacity of 36. They were classified as the DON type and another 49 were built in 1935. Two years or so later, 44 of the petrol-engined ONs were fitted with the Company's new 8-litre K-type diesel engine and redesignated CON type; they retained 38 seats. Bodywork on the ON-series buses was by Short Bros or Brush and many were modernised by Nudd Bros & Lockyer or Hooton in the early postwar period. Number **1615 (AHA 510)** - here carrying its pre-1944 bonnet number 510 - was withdrawn in 1950 for scrap, although its body was rebuilt by Nudd and mounted on to the chassis of CON No. 1523, surviving into 1956. This picture was taken at Glasshouse Street, Nottingham, in August 1940.

Above: A comparison of BMMO single- and double-decker front ends. Number **1714 (AHA 549)** was from a batch of 49 DONs built in 1935 (AHA 537-75/7-86) and is seen after rebuild by Nudd. Alongside, No. **2260 (FHA 242)** is from a batch of 50 FEDDs (FHA 200-21/3-50) with forward-entrance Brush bodywork supplied in 1938/9. All but one were renovated by Hooton - this one in 1951. These two buses survived with Midland Red until 1956 and 1960 respectively and were photographed at Leicester, St Margaret's, in August 1955.

In scenes from the mid nineteen-fifties, CON and DON buses of two decades earlier are contrasted with the then current generation of Midland Red service bus. The picture above, taken in Leicester in October 1953 has **1715** (**AHA 550**), a 1935 Short Bros-bodied DON 36-seater, alongside 1952 S13 **3954** (**OHA 954**), a Nudd Bros-bodied 40 seater. The DON had been rebuilt by Hooton in 1952 and was withdrawn in 1956. **1626** (**AHA 521**), seen below, was an ON that had been converted to CON type with BMMO diesel engine; another Hooton renovation in 1952 and also withdrawn in 1956, it ran for a showman until 1959. In this March 1955 view in Coventry, its postwar companion was S9 *(see page 41)* No. **3425** (**LHA 425**).

After withdrawal from service, Midland Red vehicles seldom found further use in a public service role, in sharp contrast with, for example, former London Transport vehicles, though some were to be seen up and down the country working for fairground showmen - that once fertile source of interesting buses. An IM6 of 1933 is seen *(above)* at Nottingham Goose Fair in October 1955. The erstwhile 1447 (**HA 8323**), a Short Bros-bodied 34-seater, had been withdrawn in 1951. **AHA 587** *(below)* was the former 1642 (the first of the batch 1642-66), a Short Bros-bodied LRR coach of 1935 that had been downgraded to service bus status in 1940. It went to a showman in 1952 and was also at the Goose Fair, already looking somewhat battered, in October of that year.

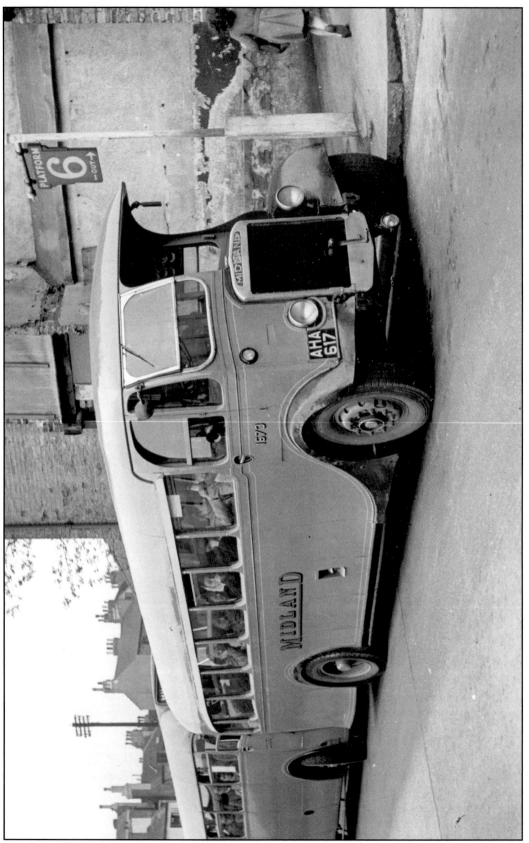

<< *Opposite page:* The SOS OLR type was a touring coach designed and introduced as a batch of 25 in 1935, as a replacement for vehicles employed on that work that had been built in 1928-30. With BMMO 6.373-litre petrol engines, forward-control configuration and Short Bros 29-seat bodies, they were very luxurious, their specification perhaps let down only by the opening canvas roof, although the latter were no doubt appreciated by clients on hot days during a tour. As with the LRR type *(see pages 16/7)*, the OLRs were downgraded for use as service buses in 1941/2: they became 34-seaters with fixed roofs and were rebuilt to forward control, as shown by **1673 (AHA 617)**, photographed in Mount Street, Nottingham, in April 1950. The vehicle was withdrawn in 1951.

Above: The SOS FEDD, produced in some quantity between 1933 and 1939, was a forward-entrance double-decker. Although the REDDs already in service had rear entrances, Midland Red's large fleet of forward-entrance single-deckers made it logical to introduce a similar entrance arrangement for the larger-capacity vehicles. The FEDD was the last double-decker built under the SOS name and well over 300 were produced. In 1935/6 there was a batch of 135 with Metro-Cammell 56-seat, metal-framed bodies, all petrol-engined but converted to diesel in 1943-7. **1774 (BHA 329)**, seen here at St Margaret's bus station, Leicester, in March 1953, was withdrawn in 1956 and was last seen on a building site in Coventry in 1962.

Above: Another view of FEDD **1774** (**BHA 329**), some 2½ years later in August 1955, again at St Margaret's, Leicester. Alongside was **3005** (**HHA 606**), a 1947 40-seat S6.

Below: **1874** (**BHA 833**) in an October 1953 view at St Margaret's. Some of the FEDDs, when converted to diesel, received AEC 7.7-litre engines, but 1874 was one of those that were fitted with the BMMO K-type unit, in this case in 1943. Withdrawn in 1956, this vehicle went on to run for a fairground showman.

Above: Another 1936 Metro-Cammell-bodied FEDD in another August 1955 view at Leicester St Margaret's. **1807 (BHA 351)** had recently emerged from overhaul and repaint. It had also been the recipient of an BMMO K-type diesel engine, though somewhat later, in 1947. The bus was withdrawn in 1957.

Below: A batch of 50 FEDDs in 1938 had Brush composite bodywork to a revised design incorporating a smoother frontal profile, also with 56 seats. All were renovated by Hooton in 1950/1, this one - **2140 (EHA 272)** - in 1951. It was withdrawn in 1960. This picture was taken at the Old Bus Station, Grantham, in June 1950.

Above: A similar group of 50 Brush-bodied FEDDs came later in 1938, delivery spilling over into 1939. A new radiator style, introduced on four units of the previous batch, was featured on these buses. It had perhaps been inspired by AEC's contemporary, though much neater, design. The batch was 2219-68, of which **2260** (**FHA 242**) is seen at St Margaret's, Leicester, in August 1955. Renovated by Hooton in 1951, it was withdrawn in 1960 *(see also page 19)*.

Below: Nineteen-thirty-nine saw the final batch of 50 FEDDs - 2332-81 - again bodied by Brush as 56-seaters. All were renovated by Hooton in 1950/1 except for one each dealt with by Carlyle and Nudd Bros. **2336** (**FHA 840**) was at the Bull Ring, Birmingham, in 1950.

The 1937 SOS SLR-type coaches had similar running units to those of the normal-control OLRs of 1935, but were forward-control 30-seaters with coachwork by English Electric to full-front and concealed radiator configuration. Their SOS petrol engines were replaced with Leyland 7.4-litre diesel units in 1947/8. **2012 (CHA 994)**, at Glasshouse Street, Nottingham, in August 1940 *(above)*, was fully modified for running after dark in blackout conditions, with white additions to the livery, masked headlamps and reduced-aperture sidelamps. **2000 (CHA 982)** *(below)*, in an August 1953 Leicester view, reveals detail changes caused by the postwar rebuilding of the entire class. All the SLRs were withdrawn in 1955.

In the period 1935-40, and to some extent matching the introduction of the FEDD as the standard double-decker, the SOS SON type set a new standard for the single-deck fleet. There were many detail differences among the various batches and in another pair from the priceless series of wartime views at Glasshouse Street, Nottingham, in the summer of 1940, **2317 (FHA 472)** *(<< opposite page)*, one of a batch of 38 of 1939, and **2390 (GHA 309)** *(above)*, one of the last batch of 50 delivered in 1940, display the rounded styling of the Brush 38-seat bodywork as well as the new style of radiator. From the second, 1937, batch (of 100) English Electric-bodied examples, **2083 (DHA 701)** *(below)* has the earlier radiator and is seen in postwar livery in September 1952.

In this pair of postwar pictures taken in Leicester in April 1955 and Loughborough in September 1950, 1940 SONs **2386** (**GHA 305**) and **2390** (**GHA 309**) *(see also page 29)* demonstrate the difference in appearance wrought by the rebuilding of most of the GHA-registered SONs with rubber-mounted windows and separate sliding ventilators. The rebuilding work on 2390 had been carried out by Nudd Bros earlier in 1950 and the vehicle was still shiny in its new coat of paint.

Another contrasting pair of photographs, taken respectively in February 1954 and November 1956 at St Margaret's bus station, Leicester, again shows unrebuilt and rebuilt examples of the SON class, this time of CHA-registered vehicles from the first production batch, of 65 (1877-1941), bodied by English Electric and delivered in 1936. **1908 (CHA 532)** *(above)* had an in-house body rebuild by BMMO soon after the war, which did little to alter its external appearance. It was withdrawn in 1955 and noted with a showman in 1959. Number **1933 (CHA 557)** *(below)* was more extensively rebuilt in 1951 by Hooton, who shared with BMMO and Nudd Bros the renovation work on bodies of this batch.

Above: The second batch of SON buses, totalling 100, was supplied in 1937/8, filling the numbers 2019-118, and again had English Electric bodywork. Whilst many bodies of other batches of SONs were renovated by outside contractors, as discussed in earlier pages, none of this batch is recorded as having been so treated and all survived in substantially original condition. **2058 (DHA 676)**, seen at St Margaret's in September 1952, was withdrawn the following year. By then it undoubtedly looked archaic but it appeared to be in sound condition, especially so for an unrebuilt 15-year-old.

Below: The final SOS-designed vehicle for coaching duties was the diesel-engined (BMMO 8-litre K-type), Duple-bodied ONC type of 1939. Built with 30 seats, the batch of 25 (2269-93) became 31-seaters in 1951. **2280 (FHA 412)** was withdrawn in 1959. Loaned to Black & White in that year to help out with summer demand, FHA 412 was later noted converted as a mobile shop in Tamworth. It was photographed at Victoria coach station, London, in September 1956.

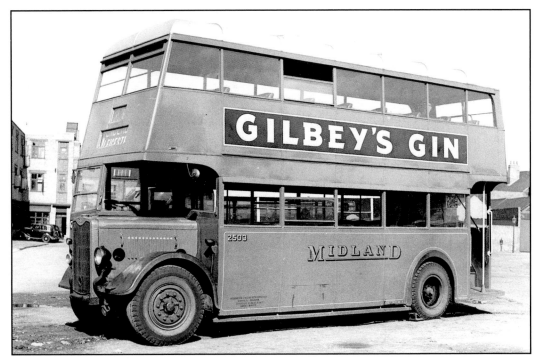

There was nothing unusual, following the outbreak of war in September 1939, in Midland Red soon having to accept Guy and Daimler chassis, with bodywork from various manufacturers, built to designs based on the Ministry of Supply's spartan, utilitarian wartime specification, though perhaps it was more of a culture shock to a company so wedded to producing its own vehicles of such individual style than it was for most others, used as the latter were to ordering from outside suppliers. Representing the Guy Arab in original condition is **2503 (GHA 927)** *(above)*, delivered in 1943 with 56-seat bodywork by Weymann, of Addlestone, pictured at Leicester in August 1948. The following year's Daimler CWA6 **2533 (GHA 968)** *(below)* had a Duple body, also a 56-seater. It was at Moseley, Birmingham, in September 1948.

There was much rebuilding work on the wartime utility buses. Many of the bodies suffered from the use of green (unseasoned) timber in their original construction and without substantial renovation would not have survived very far into the nineteen-fifties. In this pair of New Street, Birmingham, photographs taken in May 1956, an example each of the Weymann - **2512** (**GHA 936**) *(above)* - and Duple - **2534** (**GHA 969**) *(below)* - bodied Daimler CWA6s is seen after rebuilding by Willowbrook. Visually, the work inspired mixed feelings among observers, perhaps the most controversial feature being the built-in nearside-front mudguard assembly. GHA 936, unusually, found further service, with Ledgard, of Armley. It was scrapped in 1962. GHA 969 was withdrawn in 1956.

In 1949-51 the Guy Arabs with Weymann wartime bodies were rebuilt by Carlyle or Brush to a similar appearance as that of the Willowbrook-rebuilt Daimlers. **2497** and **2550** (**GHA 921/HHA 2**), both dealt with by Brush in 1950, show the somewhat "different" appearance of these rebuilds at Leicester St Margaret's in October 1950. Both buses were withdrawn in 1956.

Guy Arabs originally bodied to wartime specification by Northern Counties were somewhat less austere, as 1945 deliveries, and were regarded as being of "relaxed utility specification". Although also eventually rebuilt, they required a less severe rehabilitation. The work was done by Hooton, and the main difference from the more drastic rebuilds lay in the windows, which were not replaced with rubber-mounted fitments. **2586/7** (**HHA 81/2**) show the difference in these 1952/3 pictures at Leicester. These buses were withdrawn in 1956 (2586) and 1957.

There was much experimental work on both chassis and body design in the mid 1930s. Four SOS REC types were built in 1935/6; the type-letters stood for "**R**ear **E**ngined **C**oach", despite only one of the four having been bodied as a coach. The design incorporated a transversely mounted rear engine, with two radiators - one at each side - and positioned the driver ahead of the set back front axle allowing close supervision on passenger entry and exit on the front-entrance versions. The vehicles had a short life and were dismantled early in the war, parts from them being reused in contemporary developments. **1942 (CHA 1)** had been the solitary coach in the REC quartet, and in 1942 its chassis was reconstructed to include a horizontally mounted BMMO 8-litre K-type diesel engine; it then had transferred to it the extensively rebuilt 1936 Carlyle 40-seat bus body formerly carried by CHA 2, another of the RECs. In the new model identification system introduced in 1945, using the pefixes "S" and "D" respectively for single- and double-deckers, CHA 1 was designated S2 and it pointed the way clearly towards Midland Red's postwar styling for single-deck service buses. It is seen in its final condition, a few months before withdrawal, at Southgate Street garage, Leicester, in November 1956.

The development work in the war years, of which CHA 1 in its 1942 form was one of the results, culminated in the S6 single-decker, an underfloor-engined chassis with the K-type diesel engine. A batch of 100, 3000-99 with one-out-of-step registrations HHA 601-700, was supplied in the latter part of 1946 and 1947. The 40-seat bodywork came from Brush and Metro-Cammell (50 each) and **3089 (HHA 690)** *(above)* was one of the Brush versions. A change in regulations allowed for longer buses, and the S6s were lengthened to 29ft 3ins, allowing an increase in seating capacity to 44. The work was done by Charles H Roe, Crossgates, Leeds in 1953 and **3015 (HHA 616)** is seen below at Roe's works in the course of being converted in May of that year.

In the early postwar period the Company could not find the capacity to build new double-deckers because of its major commitment in renewing its single-deck fleet. Double-deckers were nonetheless in as much need of replacement and 100 AEC Regent II chassis with 7.7-litre engines and crash gearboxes were ordered. In another "only one adrift" numbering exercise, the batch 3100-99, known as the AD2 class, was registered JHA 1-100. 3100-49 were bodied by Brush, 3150-99 by Metro-Cammell, all as 56-seaters, and all were delivered between 1948 and 1950. One of each type, **3125** (**JHA 26**) *(Brush - above)* and the last of them, **3199** (**JHA 100**) *(Metro-Cammell - below)* are seen at St Margaret's, Leicester in February 1950 and October 1953. These buses were withdrawn in 1962 and 1963.

Above: Meanwhile, coaches were also needed, and a revised version of the S6 bus chassis was produced, incorporating an overdrive gearbox and altered back-axle ratio. Known as the C1 class, there were 45, built in 1948/9; the batch was 3300-44, registered KHA 300-44. Duple centre-entrance 30-seat coachwork was fitted. Typical of them was **3315 (KHA 315)**, seen at Llandudno in August 1959. It was withdrawn in July 1964.

Below: Twelve further coaches to similar design followed in 1950 as the C2 class. Intended for extended tours work, the C2s had only 26 seats when new, though nine of them were altered to 30 in 1954. Three of the C2s were modernised in 1959; a fourth, **3345 (KHA 345)** seen here at Digbeth in August 1962, was similarly restyled in 1961. It was withdrawn in 1966.

In the period 1948-51 single-deckers in classes S8 to S12 inclusive were produced. The photographer was able to pay a visit to the Brush works at Loughborough in May 1949 when a batch of 100 S9 40-seaters was being bodied. As with the slightly earlier batch of 100 Metro-Cammell-bodied S8s, body styling generally resembled that of the S6, although there were differences of minor detail. In the upper view can be seen **3421/15 (LHA 421/15)** whilst below are, from left to right, **3419/27/13/31 (LHA 419/27/13/31)** and an unidentified example. All 100 were extended by Roe in 1952 to become 44-seaters.

Above: The S10 class of 154 single-deckers (3577-693/5-702/4-32) was supplied in 1949/50 and was again similar to its predecessors. The 40-seat bodies were built by Brush or Metro-Cammell, but not in neat batches of fleet numbers. **3658 (NHA 658)** was by Brush and was withdrawn in 1964. It was photographed in Mount Street, Nottingham, in October 1953. The S10s also followed earlier buses in being lengthened as 44-seaters by Roe, in this case in 1952/3.

Below: The S12s - 3733-76 - came in 1950/1 and were built with longer bodies seating 44, in accordance with the recently changed regulations. They were again bodied by either Brush or Metro-Cammell, and again irregularly in terms of fleet numbers. Brush-bodied **3772 (NHA 772)** was at Leicester in 1951.

Above: **3441 (LHA 441)** was a unique member of the S9 batch 3357-456. A Brush 40-seater like the rest, dating from 1950, it was, before entering service, fitted with a Carlyle-designed front end which included electrically operated front doors. Bumpers, aluminium mouldings and a revised grille were further differences. It was at Leicester in March 1963 and was withdrawn later in the year.

Below: The 100 AECs of the AD2 class did not entirely solve the double-decker shortage, and in 1949 twenty Guy Arabs with Meadows diesel engines were purchased. Known as the GD6 class, 3357-76 had 56-seat bodies by Guy on Park Royal frames. They were later all fitted with BMMO K-type engines and were withdrawn in 1961/2. **3563 (MHA 63)** was at Dudley in August 1951.

As the 1940s gave way to the 1950s the Company was at last able to turn its attention to building its own double-deckers, the result of which was 200 D5 vehicles with BMMO 8-litre diesel engines and Brush 56-seat rear-entrance bodies. Delivered in two batches of 100 buses, the second series was fitted with platform doors and classified as the D5B type. These buses were rather heavy and a little slow with only eight litres under the bonnet; they were the last Midland Red double-deckers to be bodied by Brush. In the upper picture, still looking new and shiny, **3854** (**NHA 854**) was recently into service; it was in New Street, Birmingham in August 1951. **3864** (**NHA 864**) *(below)*, in a picture taken to illustrate the enclosed platform arrangement, was at Leicester in 1952.

The S13 class was 3877-975, supplied in 1951-3, with bodies by Carlyle, Willowbrook, Brush or Nudd Bros & Lockyer (the latter later became Duple Motor Bodies (Midland) Ltd). The bulk were 40-seat dual-purpose machines, suitable for use on both express and stage-carriage routes. **3882 (OHA 882)** in the picture above was at Southgate Street, Leicester, in September 1954. In 1956 the dual-purpose vehicles were repainted into coach livery of red with black roof and **3892 (OHA 892)** was so adorned *(below)* at Mount Street, Nottingham, in July of that year, shortly after the repainting. Both buses had Brush bodywork.

Above: The S13s comprised 99 vehicles; there should have been 100 and the last bus in the sanction turned up as the experimental chassisless LA type, **3977 (OHA 977)**. Its design largely followed that of the S13, but incorporated a number of new features. It seems to have been used as a test bed for various types of engine, having been powered in turn by BMMO 10.5-litre, Leyland 5.75-litre and BMMO 8-litre units. It had a short life for a Midland Red vehicle, being delicensed after less than ten years and sold for scrap in 1961. This Birmingham view of it dates from August 1951.

Below: The double-deck design moved on to the D7 in 1953-7, the first batch of 100 being represented by **4085 (THA 85)** at Leicester in October 1953. The D7 was the first BMMO design to lightweight standards and the 58-seat bodies were by Metro-Cammell, based on the latter's "Orion" design then recently put on to the market.

The eighth type in the postwar double-deck series was the LD8. Barely keeping pace with its needs, the Company ordered 100 Leyland PD2/20 Titans to supplement its own production. The complete bus was built at Leyland, the bodies being 56-seaters with enclosed platforms and doors. The batch was 3978-4077 and our views are of **4037/49 (SHA 437/49)** taken respectively at Southgate Street, Leicester, in August 1954 and at Coventry in March 1955. The panelling enclosing the radiator was specified by Midland Red and Leyland subsequently used it on buses for other operators. Withdrawals took place from 1965 to 1967. Some, including 4037, which went on to PVS Contracts, Upminster, found further service and one has survived in preservation.

The first 30ft-long coach design from Midland Red appeared in 1953 in two variations, C3 and C4; they were similar in appearance to the earlier, shorter C1 and C2 types. The C4s comprised a prototype bodied by Carlyle followed by a batch of eleven with Alexander 32-seat centre-entrance coachwork, typified *(above)* by **4244 (UHA 244)** at Nottingham in June 1956. 4244 was withdrawn in January 1966. Of the 63 C3 coaches (4179-241), originally bodied by Willowbrook, 17 were rebodied in 1962/3 by Plaxton as front-entrance 36-seaters. This was an unusual move for Midland Red, and the resulting vehicles were undeniably handsome, as shown by **4237 (UHA 237)**, seen at Minehead *(below)* in June 1965. This coach was withdrawn in August 1970.

The S14 prototype was unveiled in 1954. A chassisless vehicle with independent front suspension, it was the result of development work that built on experience gained with the S5 and LA types. The prototype took the number **4178** and was registered **THA 778**. It is seen *(above)* at Mount Street, Nottingham, in October 1955. It was a Carlyle-bodied 44-seater, although this was reduced to 40 in 1958, and it was withdrawn in January 1967. Between 1954 and 1959 production vehicles totalled 219, but there were many variations of greater or lesser detail: some 30 were noted in the first batch (4254-352) alone. From that batch we illustrate **4267** (**UHA 267**) *(below)* at St Margaret's, Leicester, in March 1956. It was withdrawn in July 1968 and all had gone by 1971.

Midland Red gained immense publicity when it unveiled Britain's first coaches designed specifically for high-speed running. They ran between London and Birmingham using the M1 Motorway. The C5/CM5/CM5T family of coaches appeared over the years 1958 to 1961. They were 37-seaters or 34 if fitted with a toilet compartment (the CM5Ts). These two Llandudno views from August 1959 and August 1961 show **4785 (785 GHA)** *(above)* and **4832 (832 HHA)** *(below)*, both in their first weeks of service. 4785 was withdrawn in 1971 and passed to Margo, London SW16; 4832 was one of the C5s to be converted to CM5 specification, in this case in April 1963. It was withdrawn and sold to a scrap dealer in February 1971.

4840 (EJF 668) was a Guy Arab with Gardner 5LW engine and Northern Counties 56-seat highbridge bodywork dating from 1948. It was No. 26 in the fleet of Kemp & Shaw Ltd., of Leicester, and was one of eight vehicles acquired and numbered 4838-45 when that business was taken over on 1st January 1959. Interestingly, BMMO chassis numbers (of their in-house-built vehicles) equated to their fleet numbers, hence they did not use chassis numbers 4838-45. EJF 668 was withdrawn in 1961.

The Kemp & Shaw operation had been owned by Midland Red since 1955 but was retained as a separate subsidiary with the vehicles in Kemp & Shaw livery. In Midland Red ownership, a wartime Guy Arab was withdrawn, and the eight vehicles referred to on the previous page were merged into the main fleet when Kemp & Shaw was liquidated on 1st January 1959. They consisted of six more Guys and two Leyland Titans. **JBC 989**, which took Midland Red fleet number **4845**, was a 1952 Leyland PD2/12 Titan. It had been Kemp & Shaw No. 31 and its highbridge Leyland body was a 56-seater. It was withdrawn in May 1967 and sold for scrap the following month. These pictures of it were taken at Derby in May 1959.

Kemp & Shaw **GRY 763** had been new in 1950. It was a lowbridge Leyland-bodied 53-seat Titan PD2/1 which lasted with Midland Red until June 1967, when it was sold to a Birmingham PSV driving school. In the view above it is seen at Derby in August 1960 with its Midland Red fleet number **4844**, and below, in March 1957 at St Margaret's, Leicester, in original livery (but BMMO ownership) as Kemp & Shaw No. **30**.

Soon after the Kemp & Shaw absorption, Midland Red took over another Leicestershire operator, H Boyer & Son, of Rothley, on 1st February 1959. The rare event of second-hand vehicles being retained and used in the Midland Red fleet was repeated when three Boyer vehicles - two Sentinels and a Leyland Royal Tiger - were repainted and put into service. The numbers 4846-8 were allocated to the ex-Boyer vehicles of which Sentinel STC6 **4847** (**GUT 543**) is shown above and **4848** (**HJU 546**), the Leyland-bodied Royal Tiger, below. The latter was sold to Stevenson, Spath, in April 1966. These are both Leicester views.

Between 1958, when the prototype D9 72-seat double-decker appeared, and 1966 when the last production version appeared, no fewer than 345 of this advanced and efficient machine entered the Midland Red fleet. Variations of both the production vehicles when compared with the prototype and within the various production batches were too numerous to attempt a listing, for scarcely any two were exactly alike - they all had power steering and two-pedal transmission, though, features among those so appreciated at Northampton during the encounter described in the Introduction. **4933 (933 KHA)** *(above)* was from the first production batch and was new in July 1961, whilst **4976 (2976 HA)** *(below)* was from the second batch in April 1962. Both were photographed in Leicester.

Along with many other operators, Midland Red was not tempted into investing in early, unreliable rear-engined double-deckers from proprietary manufacturers, but was nonetheless impressed by the high-capacity concept. The solution was the D10, an underfloor-engined 10.5-litre machine. There were two prototypes in 1960/1, which in the event were not succeeded by any production versions. The second of them was a two-door, twin-staircase 65-seater and the first, which is illustrated, was a single-door 78-seater. Quite why the design never went into production is not known. Geoffrey Atkins's pictures of **4943** (**943 KHA**) were taken at Victoria Embankment, Nottingham, after the vehicle had been sold into preservation.

Midland Red ordered 100 Leopard PSU3/4 chassis from Leyland Motors for 1962/3 delivery. The bodywork was to the BET Federation style, though fitted out to Midland Red requirements. Weymann, of Addlestone, and Willowbrook, of Loughborough, shared the coachbuilding contract, both providing 53-seat service bus bodies with Willowbrook also supplying some 48-seat dual-purpose machines. The latter were painted in the red and black livery and one of them, **5182 (5182 HA)** is seen *(above)* at Canning Circus, Nottingham, in June 1963, a week or so after its May delivery into the fleet. The Weymann service bus version is epitomised by **5168 (5168 HA)** *(below)*, spotted at Nottingham Forest having conveyed people to the Goose Fair in October 1968.

The new regulations concerning overall dimensions allowed Midland Red, in 1962, to introduce a 36ft-long single-decker and by 1966 a substantial fleet of such vehicles had been produced, and given the class identities S16, S17, S19 and S21A, in which many features of earlier designs were evident. The S17 variant was built from 5446 in 1963 to 5773 in late 1966 and is represented by **5732** (**EHA 732D**) *(above)*, photographed at The Newarke, Leicester, in June 1968. It had entered service in September 1967 and the 52-seat bodywork structure was by Carlyle, finished by Plaxton, of Scarborough. Three vehicles built in 1966 were dual-purpose 48-seaters initially classified S21A, later S22 and finally S17, when they were converted to 52-seaters for driver-only operation. Number **5723** (**DHA 723C**), in S22 mode, was in the same place in October 1968. 5732 passed to the West Midlands PTE; 5723 was withdrawn in June 1977 and sold for scrap.

Above: Midland Red's high-speed motorway coaching operation quickly produced a requirement for vehicles with a higher seating capacity, and from 1963 to 1966 thirty CM6 36ft-long coaches were placed in service. They ran up some very high mileages in a short life - they were withdrawn between 1972 and 1974 - and ended their days, somewhat unsuitably, on occasional stage-carriage duties. In their heyday, **5658 (BHA 658C)** was at London, Victoria, waiting to move into the coach station to take up a timing to Coventry. It is parked in the exit from Samuelson's garage, opposite the coach station, where vehicles were serviced and fuelled between journeys. As a 44-seater with a toilet compartment, 5658 was of type CM6T. It was scrapped after withdrawal in April 1974.

Below: The need for maximum-length coaches was such in the mid 1960s that 65 Leyland Leopards were acquired, classified LC7-10. Numbers 5774-822, of type LC7, had 49-seat Duple Commander coachwork. Brand new **5800 (CHA 100C)** was at Victoria coach station in September 1965.

Above: There was only one member of Midland Red's LC8 class. **5823 (CHA 123C)** was a 30ft-long Leyland Leopard L2T, it carried Plaxton Panorama 36-seat coachwork and was intended for use on extended tours. New in July 1965, it lasted just a decade and was sold in July 1975 to a dealer who disposed of it to Leeds City Council, with whom it was used on school duties until sold for scrap in December 1984. In this November 1969 view it was inside St Margaret's garage, Leicester.

Below: Fifteen more 30ft-long Leopards, of type PSU4/4R, became class LC9 in 1966. Plaxton 36-seat coachwork was again specified - an updated version of the Panorama - for extended tours. **5836 (GHA 336D)** was at Perth on its way to the Shetland Isles in July 1971. Withdrawn in December 1976, it reappeared in April 1978 converted as a towing vehicle.

Above: The Leyland Leopard contingent was augmented in 1966 when ten PSU3/4R versions appeared in the fleet. Designated LS20, they were fitted with Willowbrook dual-purpose 49-seat bodywork, which conformed to the then current BET Federation design. 5839-48 were stored for some months before entering service in March and April 1967. Brand new **5844 (JHA 844E)** was at Mount Street, Nottingham, in May 1967. It was scrapped after withdrawal in November 1980.

Below: The last BMMO-built buses were a series of 36ft-long single-deckers of types S21-3 built in 1967-70. Based on well-established BMMO practice, they were similar to the earlier S17s. **5855 (JHA 855E)** was one of a batch of 30 (5849-78) S21s, with BMMO dual-purpose 49-seat bodywork. It was photographed using a temporary terminus for the X99 service, in Park Row, Nottingham, in July 1968.

Above: The S21 was closely followed by 37 of the S22 type, which were dual-purpose 45-seaters fitted for driver-only operation. The batch was 5879-915 and **5894 (MHA 894F)** is seen in Leicester in June 1968, two months after entering service. When not yet ten years old, it was withdrawn and scrapped.

Below: The very last BMMO production programme was for 76 driver-only operated, 51-seat service buses: the S23 class. Numbers 5916-41 were the last buses to be entirely built by BMMO - 5941 entered service in January 1970 - and partially built 5942-91 were completed by Plaxton. One of the latter group, **5966 (UHA 966H)**, was at Leicester in January 1971. This one was scrapped in 1980.

Thus ended - with these 1967-70 BMMO-designed S21, S22 and S23 vehicles - a successful in-house vehicle-production operation, which over a period of almost a half-century had managed, despite premises and facilities that were frankly not the match of those enjoyed by the proprietary manufacturers, to keep the Birmingham & Midland Motor Omnibus Company at the forefront of bus and coach design in the United Kingdom. From the first SOS in 1923, through the rear- and underfloor-engined designs to the advanced integral and lightweight buses of the later years, and culminating in the magnificent motorway coaches, which - when such things were allowed - were easily capable of wafting passengers silently and comfortably to London at 100mph, Midland Red-built public service vehicles were something of which the Company was justifiably proud; as the man said: *"Wish we had some of them..."*

Above: The failure, for whatever reason, to pursue the D10 (a parallel here with London Transport and the FRM, perhaps...) led to Midland Red seeking high-capacity double-deckers elsewhere, and the Daimler Fleetline was chosen. Large numbers entered service from 1963 to 1968 as types DD11 and DD12. Fifty arrived in 1963; they had Gardner 6LX engines and Alexander 77-seat bodywork and were the DD11 type. The DD12s - Nos 5992-6140 - came in 1966-8 and were very similar. **6085** (**JHA 85E**) is representative of the DD12s; it was at Leicester St Margaret's in September 1969.

Below: From 1969 to 1971 further Fleetlines, generally similar but to dual-doorway 75-seat specification, came into the fleet as the DD13 class. A 1969 example was **6165 (SHA 865G)**, also at St Margaret's in September 1969.

On 1st January 1969, Midland Red became part of the National Bus Company. It would be some time before there was any great evidence of consequent change, and 1970's 30 Plaxton-bodied Leyland Leopards - of type PSU3A/4R, forming BMMO class LC11 - were reassuringly still red when they arrived in May-August. Although neither built nor bodied by BMMO, and soon afterwards to be repainted in the NBC's scarcely imaginative all-over white corporate coaching livery, they are a positive note upon which to round off this retrospective of the mighty Midland Red. The batch was 6226-55 and we illustrate **6231/8 (WHA 231/8H)** at St Margaret's garage, Leicester, and at Betws-y-Coed, both in September 1972.